# Old Bankfoot and Waterloo

## David Pettigrew

An 1898 view looking north towards Bankfoot from the Perth Road (today the B867). The field on the left now contains the town's bowling green and tennis courts and also the houses of Nicoll Place and Nicoll Drive. Cairneyhill Road is going up the hill on the right. In the background are the chimney and buildings of Airleywight Linen Works on Prieston Road. Note the old-fashioned hayricks to their right.

© David Pettigrew, 2023
First published in the United Kingdom, 2023,
by Stenlake Publishing Ltd.
www.stenlake.co.uk
ISBN 978-1-84033-946-8

The publishers regret that they cannot supply copies of any pictures featured in this book.

Printed by
P2D Books, 1 Newlands Rd,
Westoning, Bedford MK45 5LD

## Acknowledgements

The author wishes to thank the Local History Librarian of the A. K. Bell Library, Perth, for his assistance.

## Further Reading

The following were the principal books and websites used by the author during his research.

Thomas Brown, *The Parish of Auchtergaven: The History of Bankfoot*, 2000 (self-published).
Don Cumming, *Guide to Auchtergaven and Neighbourhood*, 1894.
Rev. J.C. Gordon, 'The Parish of Auchtergaven' (1963), in *The Third Statistical Account of Scotland: The Counties of Perth and Kinross*, 1979.
Robert Grieves, *Wheels Around Perthshire*, 2009.
Val Honeyman, ''A Very Dangerous Place'?: Radicalism in Perth in the 1790s', *The Scottish Historical Review*, October 2008.
Alistair F. Nisbet, 'The Bankfoot Light Railway', *Backtrack* magazine, July 2010.
Peter R. Paul, *Views of Bankfoot and Vicinity*, no date.
Robin Smith, *The Making of Scotland*, 2001.
TheCourier.co.uk
*Daily Record*
*Dundee Courier*
*Evening Telegraph*
*The Scotsman*
*Leslie's Directory for Perth and Perthshire 1911-12*
Auchtergaven golf course: golfsmissinglinks.co.uk
Bankfoot Church Centre: bankfootchurch.org
Bankfoot Inn: www.bankfootinn.co.uk
Historic Environment Scotland: www.historicenvironment.scot
Imperial War Museum: www.iwm.org.uk
Places of Worship in Scotland: www.scottishchurches.org.uk
Presbytery of Perth: www.perthpresbytery.org.uk

Bankfoot Station.

# Introduction

Bankfoot is within the parish of Auchtergaven which derives from the Gaelic uachdar-gamhainn: 'upland of the yearling cattle'. A community had been established at least by the 1500s and was marked as 'Preestoun' on a map of the parish from 1600. At that time it had three mills. In 1681 it became a Burgh of Barony, which conferred the right to hold a weekly market. By the end of the eighteenth century the parish was holding five annual fairs, though this had reduced to two by the late 1800s.

In the early nineteenth century the road past the then recently-completed church was improved for coaching traffic (later becoming the A9). Today's Bankfoot emerged along this route from 1815, including the houses of Waterloo, named after the battle which took place that year. By the late 1800s services included an inn, a post office with savings bank, money order and telegraph facilities, a school, many shops, as well as the linen works which was a major employer. Bankfoot was connected to the railway network in 1906.

The population of the parish steadily rose from 1,677 in 1755 to a high of 3,417 in 1831. It then fluctuated over succeeding decades but generally fell and the number of inhabitants in 2016 was 1,220, reflecting the decrease in local industry. The linen works and other businesses closed in the twentieth century and the number of shops also reduced. Around 1900 Bankfoot enjoyed the services of no less than three bakers, seven grocers, two drapers, two boot shops, one boot repairer, two tailors, a stationer, a cycle repair shop, six tea shops or cafes, three hotels, and one restaurant. By 1963 most of these had been replaced by travelling vans and there were only eight shops left.

In more recent years, with the addition of new housing, Bankfoot has settled into existence as a dormitory town and many locals travel to Perth and further afield for work. Surrounded by beautiful countryside, it remains a very pleasant place to live.

The interior of the parish church in 1907. It had been refurbished and remodelled in 1899 and could seat 1,200 parishioners. The pipe organ was installed in 1906.

The New Inn appears on the Ordnance Survey map of 1867 and was still carrying that name on the OS map ninety years later. At some point in the twentieth century it was also known as Hunter's Lodge and it stood on the Perth Road, just opposite the junction with the road to Moneydie. The site is now taken by modern houses. The inn was briefly visited by Queen Victoria on 7 September 1842 during her first visit to Scotland; she enjoyed refreshments and recorded in her diary that the place gave her her first sight of the Highlands. Other famous visitors to Bankfoot have included Sir Walter Scott, the painter Sir John Millais, the Crown Prince of Japan in 1901, and Queen Elizabeth II. Jimmy Shand and his band played at the church hall.

By the 1890s Bankfoot had become a popular destination for day trippers and in 1895 locals petitioned the Highland Railway to open a line to their town. This did not come to fruition but in 1896 the Light Railways Act was passed and a company was formed to build a light railway from Bankfoot to join with the Caledonian Railway's Perth to Aberdeen main line at Strathord. The line and station opened on 7 May 1906, with Bankfoot residents being 'agog with excitement' according to the *Dundee Courier*. Just about every man, woman and child in town visited the new amenity and there was a great clamour for tickets – 71 lucky people got one for the first train which left at 8.10 a.m.

This photo from 1906 gives a wider view of the station's position just beyond the foot of the hill where the church stands. Alongside the station building there was a 400-foot platform, as well as a goods shed and sidings. The derrick, right of centre, was used for loading goods and there was a cattle pen on the far right. Rolling stock and power were initially supplied by the Caledonian Railway which took over the line in 1912. The Caledonian itself became part of the London, Midland and Scottish Railway during the 'Grouping' of Britain's many railway companies in 1923.

In 1907 there were five inbound and six outbound services per day and by 1925 this actually increased to eight in and out Mondays to Fridays with additional ones at the weekend. Nonetheless, passenger numbers were generally low and the station closed to them on 13 April 1931. Goods services went on for another 33 years, transporting mostly feedstuff for livestock coming in and cattle going out. Although the station is deserted in this photo from 1950, the line was particularly busy in the potato harvest seasons, with extra trains being laid on to accommodate the traffic.

Seen here in June 1936, the engine shed and water tower stood a short distance south of the station itself. In the early years the line was worked by Caledonian '171' class 0-4-4T engines which were made for light railway use. Later, good services were run by Caledonian 0-6-0s and then by locomotives that were ordinarily too heavy for a light railway. The final goods train ran on 7 September 1964 and the rails were lifted in November that year. The last porter was local man Danny Douglas. Later, a caravan park took the site before the houses of Innewan Gardens were built.

In this photo the roof of the station building is behind the hut in the centre. Overlooking both is Auchtergaven Parish Church, its original name, which was likely to have been the third church building on this site, the first being built in 1567 (other sources say a church has been there since the tenth century). The parish church was built in 1812/13 by John Stewart of Dunkeld, with the tower – a gift from the Duke of Atholl – added in the early 1900s. It had a Dutch-made bell which dated from 1757. The church became that of Auchtergaven and Moneydie when these two parishes united in 1979.

A closer view of the church which shows its stained-glass windows. The war memorial on the right was unveiled by the Duke of Atholl on 6 March 1921 during what was described by the *Perthshire Advertiser* as a 'beautiful and solemn little ceremony'. On its bronze plaques there are the names of one civilian and 77 military fatalities of the First World War and one civilian and eight military fatalities of the Second World War. The plaque showing those lost in the latter conflict was unveiled by Lady Abertay of Tullybelton on 10 November 1946.

The junction of Cairneyhill Road and Main Street with Prieston Road running along the right of the photograph. In the foreground is the unusual turnstyle which gave access to the path to the war memorial. The gates and turnstyle were *in situ* and well maintained until at least 2009, though they had gone by 2016 and only the two outside pillars remain. The houses of Nicoll Place and Nicoll Drive now take up the field on the left.

A view of Bankfoot looking west from the parish church tower, 1925. Dominating the centre of the view is Airelywight Linen Works on Prieston Road. This factory replaced houses on the site and also a chapel of the United Secession Church. It has itself since been replaced by the houses of Graham Court. Auchtergaven South United Free Church (see page 34), which still stands, can be seen at the upper right. In the upper left, at the end of Prieston Road, is the school.

Another view from the tower, looking north-west and showing the houses and back gardens of Main Street. To the north, prominent in the centre background, is the hill of Craig Obney, 403 metres above sea level. This was once the site of a Pictish hill fort and parts of its walls can still be seen.

Main Street (Dunkeld Road), 1896. The Bankfoot Inn, with its wooden porch, is on the right. As Bankfoot developed on the main road to the north, the inn was established as a coaching stop in the 1760s and had stables behind. When it was built, the inn stood on its own but more houses were built on the street from 1790.

A later view of the inn, by which time the stone portico, familiar today, had been added. According to the inn's website, the building has long been haunted by a variety of ghosts, including that of a little girl, an old woman and something known as 'the thing'. There have also been reports of mysterious voices in the laundry room and of taps turning themselves on. Apparently, in coaching times coffins from hearse coaches would be stored overnight in the stables. In 2015 the *Dundee Evening Telegraph* reported that paranormal investigators had concluded that the building is indeed haunted, with some ghosts even revealing their names, though how investigators obtained this information was not reported.

The shop on the right of this view of Main Street has long since closed; the building is now a private house and has dormer windows on the roof level. Adjacent are the cottages of Lower Piersland and Upper Piersland, also now with different upper windows (Upper Piersland has also lost a lower window), and beyond them the pub is now the premises of the Nisa Local store. After the First World War, the Bankfoot Motor Company provided bus services to the town. The company was started by a man named Nicoll but in 1925 it was taken over by brothers Alexander Stanley Whyte and James Taylor Whyte. In the 1930s two additional Sunday bus services to and from Stanley were started by Stanley-based operators Allan & Scott. From 1946 this company was taken over by A. C. McLellan of Spittalfield. In 1961 the Whyte brothers sold their company to Walter Alexander of Falkirk, who introduced new buses although services began to be reduced, a matter complained about by the parish minister in his entry for Auchtergaven in the *Third Statistical Account*. He noted how important the services were for local people but Alexander withdrew them in 1967.

James Young was listed as a grocer on Main Street in a trade directory of 1903. Like many houses on the road, this has since been given an upper level and is now a private house.

While this three-storey building remains prominent towards the north of Main Street, the building contains flats and the 'Fish Restaurant' is long gone.

The Atholl Hotel – now simply The Atholl – is on the right of this view looking north. In the 1860s it was known as the Athole Tavern. The chimney of the town's gasworks is on the left; these were providing gas lighting to the town from at least 1882. In 1907 they were run by Robert Young. A smithy was also in this vicinity, a little further up the street from the gasworks; by the 1950s the latter had gone but the smithy remained.

A view looking south with the Atholl Hotel on the left. The hotel's outhouses, facing the camera, have long since been demolished. Among the buildings on the left side of the street was the single-storey post office which remained open until 2008. It is now an architect's office. In the 1960s the delivery staff comprised one full-time postman and two full-time postwomen.

Further north along Dunkeld Road, very little has changed apart from the replacement of the single-storey house in the centre of the view with an extension of the terrace. In the mid-nineteenth century there was another pub among these buildings, the Diamond Inn, and later the police station was based in the detached single-storey house. In the mid-1800s the station was housed in a building which stood further south, roughly opposite the Atholl Hotel. William Campbell was listed as the local constable in 1911-12. Bankfoot still had a policeman in the 1960s.

A view of the same position on Dunkeld Road, looking south. On the higher ground is Auchtergaven North United Free Church, now a private home.

The very last house on the road north out of Bankfoot (along with its neighbour opposite), largely unchanged today. Beyond this point, further north lay the Corral Quarry, named after the burn on which Bankfoot stands. Mentioned in the *New Statistical Account* and therefore in operation at least by the 1840s, this was open until the early part of the twentieth century and was one of a number of local quarries that produced the sandstone used to construct many of the buildings in the area. Slate quarries were also in operation and, according to Thomas Brown, Bankfoot once had a number of shoemakers in business because slate was hard on footwear and local workers constantly needed shoes repaired or replaced.

Bankfoot seen from the west around 1916. These fields are still largely intact and Bankfoot remains a country town surrounded by farmland.

Although extended, this house still stands on Dunkeld Road between Bankfoot and Waterloo. Coral Quarry was on the other side of the road. Bankfoot's first water supply came via a water main from Shenval Springs in Shochie Valley to Stanley (this stopped in 1930). Later a tank was built in the Recreation Field which was in use until 1923 when pumping was introduced from the River Tay. For a while there was also a water tank at Cowford. In 1910 a supply from Coral Quarry, where there was a large well in the workings, was introduced, pumping to a tank at Coltrannie although this proved inadequate. Finally, in 1930, Bankfoot, Stanley and Dunkeld combined to form the Dunkeld Regional Water Supply District and water was pumped from Loch Ordie, above Dunkeld. Drainage and sewers were installed in 1938 with a sewage works at Loakmill.

The hamlet of Waterloo is ranged along Dunkeld Road around a mile north of Bankfoot. It is supposedly named after the famous battle and its first houses were said to have been built either for soldiers returning from it or for widows of men who did not return. Early inhabitants were certainly likely to have been cotters and weavers.

With its old houses, even by the time of the First World War, coming to Waterloo was said to have been like 'stepping into another world'. The two cottages to the right have gone but Thornhill cottage, left of centre, remains, as does Waterloo farmhouse on the far left, also supposedly built around 1815.

Now self-catering accommodation, Waterloo farmhouse was once a berry farm which attracted travelling labourers. Berry-picking season was also a big event for locals and there was often a 'carnival atmosphere' as people came to take part.

A number of Waterloo's old cottages have gone and, while new houses have appeared, these photographs show a busier place than it is now. Very little is recorded about the community but in the early 1900s there was a grocer's shop housed in an old black bus. There was also a church and a 'white house' that housed poorer families.

Returning to the southern edge of Bankfoot, Prieston Road branches off Dunkeld Road and heads west to the area of houses known as Prieston just beyond the school and next to Tulliebelton Road. This photograph shows the houses of the road between the Airleywight linen works, just out of shot to the right, and the school on the far left. In the late 1700s there were 182 weavers and around 40 cotton spinners in the town. There were also local distilleries providing employment though these had reduced from four to two by the mid 1800s and had disappeared by the mid 1900s. John Dewar of Perth's distillery at Inveralmond employed a number of Bankfoot residents. From the 1840s the linen works became the main industrial employer in the town.

The wall and entrance to Airleywight Linen Works is in the centre of this view of Prieston Road. Established by Thomas Wylie of Airleywight House in the 1840s, the works were a major source of jobs for decades, in its own way continuing the work of Thomas's father, James, who had begun the process of improving the fortunes of Auchtergaven parish earlier in the century. In its earlier years – certainly before the Education Act of 1872 made primary education mandatory – the works employed a number of local children who started work at 10 a.m. and finished at 3 p.m., then going on to their schooling. The 'factory', as the works were known locally, later became a builder's yard, which by the 1960s had become part of a major civil engineering firm and was also a large local employer. Eventually houses were built in its place.

When this photo was taken in the early 1900s, these houses on the north side of Prieston Road looked onto open fields. While the houses are more or less unchanged the fields have since been taken by a mix of post-war local authority homes, retirement homes and other modern houses. For some time after the Second World War, the fields were also the site of an estate of 'prefab' homes. Supposedly temporary, they were still in place in the 1960s when the author of the parish entry in the *Third Statistical Account* noted, rather tartly, that they were 'assuming some quality of permanence'.

Prieston Road, 1908. The Whyte brothers' Bankfoot Motor Company had its bus garage on Prieston Road, opposite the school. From the time of the Second World War the company's fleet comprised six cream and brown Bedford buses, some of which had notoriously uncomfortable wooden seats. The company also had a workshop and petrol pumps on Main Street.

Heading north off Prieston Road, Church Lane leads to the building that was once Auchtergaven United Presbyterian Church. This was built in 1844, a year after the ecclesiastical disagreement known as the 'Disruption' caused a split in the parish church congregation – some parishioners stayed there while others went off to form this church. It was renovated and reseated by Perth-based architect William Maclaren in 1883. In 1900 the congregation united with that of the local Free Church (also created by the 'Disruption') and it became Auchtergaven South United Free Church. There was also a North U.F. Church on Dunkeld Road (now a private house; see page 22). After the congregation reunited with the parish church in 1936, the building became the parish church hall. At the time of writing the rear part of the building has become a private dwelling while the main part is undergoing renovation. In its history Bankfoot has also had a Roman Catholic church, a gospel hall, a United Secession chapel, and a 'tin kirk' used by the Episcopal Church.

The west end of Prieston Road in 1908, with the school on the far left. The junction with Newhall Street – previously called Laganallachy Street – is on the far right. This leads to Coronation Park. Previously the 'Recreation Park', this was renamed for the coronation of George VI in 1937. The park was the home of Bankfoot Athletic junior football club – nicknamed the 'Bankies' – which was formed in 1919 and lasted until 2014. Its most famous players were Paul Sturrock and Jim Weir, who went on to have illustrious careers with Dundee United and St Johnstone respectively.

Auchtergaven Public School was erected after the passing of the 1872 Education Act. An early mention of it appears in an 1878 edition of the *Dundee Courier*, which reported that the scholars presented their headmaster, Mr Monroe, with a 'handsome and valuable timepiece' on the occasion of his marriage. An oddity of the parish is that there is no town or village within it that carries the name Auchtergaven; according to the parish entry in the *Third Statistical Account* one schoolmaster attempted to change the name of the town to Auchergaven but without success. The school building, which has been extended, is still in use as Auchtergaven Primary School with a roll of 126 pupils in 2022. In 1926 the school had 181 pupils. The highest roll recorded was 231 in 1914.

Prieston Road with the public school on the right. In the foreground is the junction with the bridge over the Garry Burn, leading on to Tulliebelton Road. The Garry is one of several tributaries of the Ordie Burn, after which Strathord is named. The house on the left was later reduced in size to two upper and lower front windows, the other part being replaced by a new house. Another block of two semi-detached houses has recently been added at the end of the road, opposite the bridge in the area where the bus garage used to stand.

An 1896 photo taken from the bridge over the Garry Burn. The wall of the school where it borders the burn now has a gate allowing entry into the school grounds. Local parents today would no doubt be deeply alarmed by this rickety looking platform over the water, long since replaced with a more substantial footbridge with guard rails.

This photo was taken at the point where Prieston Road ends and becomes 'Backmill Road', leading to Airleywight House and estate and Backmill Farm.

The houses of Garry Place now stand in the area opposite the bridge, just out of shot to the right. This was where the prisoner of war camp was based in the Second World War, extending from here to the driveway of Airleywight House. The inmates were Italian soldiers who got on well with the locals, with some doing chores and odd jobs in the town. The camp was later the site of a chicken factory. Polish soldiers were also based in Bankfoot during the war and a number of them married into the community.

Backmill Farm had a corn mill and there was also a mill lade which fed into Airleywight's curling pond. Long disused and known as 'The Curly', all that is left of the pond is a clearing amongst woods. The break in the wall on the right was the opening to a track into Airleywight estate which is now the main drive to the house. Once part of the crownlands of Scotland, the land which forms the estate was gifted by William the Lion to his daughter Marjorie in the late 1100s. In 1806 it was inherited by James Wylie, who had previously been a merchant and haberdasher in Perth and in the 1790s was involved with the Perth Friends of the People, a society of 1,200 members which campaigned for parliamentary and burgh council reform. At this time the authorities were afraid of the potential spread of revolution from France and the Lord Advocate described Wylie as the 'most intemperate revolutioner in Scotland' and had his correspondence secretly intercepted. In 1792 Wylie was possibly connected with a riot in Perth, during which an effigy of Henry Dundas, the most powerful politician in Scotland, was burned. However, he avoided prosecution and although he continued to campaign for reform, he became less radical after taking possession of Airleywight.

Wylie had Airleywight House built for his family on the site of a previous house between 1810 and 1812. As a landowner, he became interested in agricultural improvements and also offered feus for house-building in Bankfoot and Waterloo. He died in 1838, 'universally respected' according to the Lord Advocate of that time, an indication of how much the authorities' attitude towards him had changed. His son Thomas inherited the estate and continued the family influence in the area by establishing the linen works on Prieston Road. In 1908 the house was destroyed in a fire but fully restored within a year. It eventually passed out of Wylie family hands and was requisitioned for military use during the Second World War (during which Luftwaffe planes twice emptied their bomb cargoes on the lands around Bankfoot, on one occasion quite close to the house). Some restoration work was carried out in the 1980s and, partially derelict, the B-listed house was fully restored by its owners in the 2010s.

In 1828 the manse of Auchtergaven Parish Church was built at the western side of the town, across the Garry Burn from the school. The building still stands, off Mansfield Park, immediately north of Bankfoot Church Centre. The rear part of the building was removed around 1960 and subsequently replaced. The manse was at the centre of an 1870 incident, referred to by the Dundee and Perthshire press as 'The Auchtergaven Case', when the minister of Auchtergaven, Mr Wight, was accused of 'fornication and indecent and scandalous familiarity' with a woman at the manse and also in a room in Perth. The woman was in fact Wight's servant, Emily Fraser, to whom he was secretly engaged. The case was brought before the Presbytery of Dunkeld, and witnesses lodging evidence against Wight included a man called Thomson, referred to by Wight's defence as 'the minister's daft man'. In spite of Thomson admitting that he was 'not always in the habit of speaking the truth', numerous testimonies to Fraser's unimpeachable character and what appears to have been vigorous local support for Wight, the presbytery found against him and he was deposed from his position.

Bankfoot from the south-west, 1896, with the road from Tulliebelton in the foreground. The public school on Prieston Road is on the immediate left and the linen works' chimney is right of centre. In the last century Tulliebelton Road has seen house building along where it branches off from Prieston Road The farm of Broompark is on the top of the hill to the right behind the parish church.

Robert Nicoll was born at Little Tullybelton, seen here, on 7 January 1814. A gifted child, it was said that he knew his alphabet by the age of 18 months. As a young man he opened a lending library in Dundee and then became a politically campaigning editor of the *Leeds Times* newspaper. He died of tuberculosis in Edinburgh in 1837, aged only 23. He only produced one collection of poems, paid for by subscription, but his work was compared favourably to that of Burns and celebrated by experts of the time. Six editions of the poems had been published by the centenary of his birth.

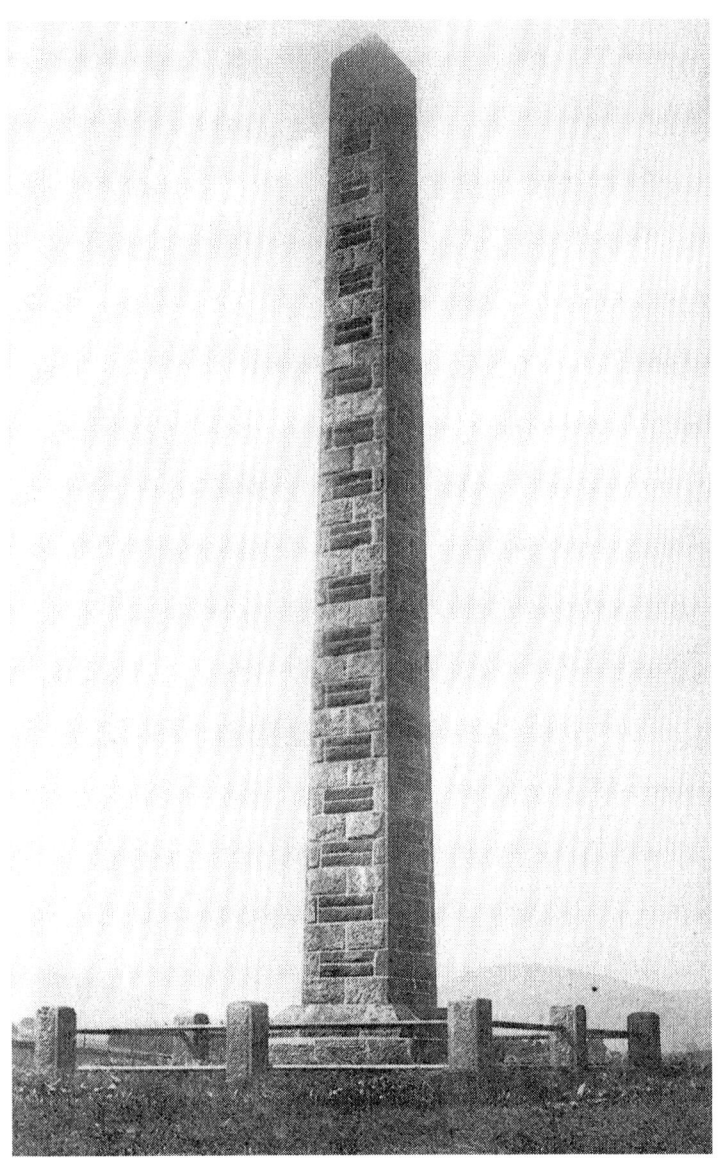

To commemorate the poet, this fifty-foot monument was erected in 1857 next to his birthplace, on ground donated by Colonel Richardson Robertson of Tullybelton estate. It was dedicated at an inauguration ceremony conducted by the Provost of Perth and attended by around a hundred people, including the poet's parents and other family members. The monument carries the inscription 'I have written my heart in my poems'. It was cleaned and restored in 1902 and in 1914 the centenary of Nicoll's birth was celebrated by locals. There was another celebration on the 150th anniversary in 1964. The poem below reflects something of Nicoll's political views

## We'll Mak' the Warld Better Yet

The braw folk crush the poor folk down,
An' blood an' tears are rinnin' het;
An' meikle ill and meikle wae,
We a' upon the earth have met.
An' falsehood aft comes boldly forth,
And on the throne of truth doth sit;
But true hearts a' — gae work awa' —
We'll mak' the warld better yet!

Though superstition, hand in hand,
W' prejudice — that gruesome hag —
Gangs linkin' still; though misers make
Their heaven o' a siller bag:
Though ignorance, wi' bloody hand,
Is tryin slavery's bonds to knit —
Put knee to knee, ye bold an' free,
We'll mak' the warld better yet!

See yonder cooff wha becks an' bows
To yonder fool wha's ca'd a lord:
See yonder gowd-bedizzen'd wight —
Yon fopling o' the bloodless sword.
Baith slave, an' lord, an' soldier too,
Maun honest grow, or quickly flit;
For freemen a', baith grit an' sma', —
We'll mak' the warld better yet!

Yon dreamer tells us o' a land
He frae his airy brain hath made —
A land where truth and honesty
Have crushed the serpent falsehood's head.
But by the names o' love and joy,
An' common-sense, and lear an' wit,
Put back to back, — and in a crack
We'll mak' our warld better yet!

The knaves and fools may rage and storm,
The growling bigot may deride —
The trembling slave away may rin,
And in his tyrant's dungeon hide;
But free and bold, and true and good,
Unto this oath their seal have set —
"Frae pole to pole we'll free ilk soul, —
The warld shall be better yet! "

There has been a house at Tullybelton since the 1500s. The Marquess of Montrose hid there for a week in 1644, while on the run from Parliamentary forces (he was a supporter of King Charles I in his conflict with the English Parliament). Later that year he led a Royalist army to victory at the Battle of Tippermuir and captured Perth for the King, although he was eventually captured and in 1650 was hanged, beheaded and dismembered at Edinburgh. The current house was built around 1850 and remodelled in 1911-12 after a fire. In the twentieth century it was the home of Charles Barrie, Baron Abertay, a merchant, shipowner and MP. He died there in 1940 and it remained in the ownership of his wife, Lady Abertay, until the 1960s. In new ownership in 2005, the house was once again upgraded and, along with its 250-acre estate, was last on the market in 2020 for £6.75 million. It was listed as having three reception rooms, a library, a billiards room, two offices, six bedrooms (the main one with adjoining 'his and hers' dressing rooms and bathrooms). In the outhouses also listed were a laundry, gym, kitchen, and a gun and fishing-rod room.

Tullybeagles Lodge was a few miles west of Bankfoot. Standing on high ground and painted white, apparently it could be seen for miles around, supposedly even from Perth. In the 1950s the lodge hosted Queen Elizabeth II for grouse shooting while she was a guest at Meikleour House. The lodge was knocked down in the 1960s.